It's Snowing in Santiago de Chuco

By Brady Rhoades

ACKNOWLEDGMENTS

Grateful acknowledgment is made to the editors of the following publications, in which the original versions of these poems first appeared.

The Amherst Review: Unfinished man
Antioch Review: It's Snowing in Santiago de Chuco, No Other Way
Baltimore Review: Stinkthing
BEAR FLAG REPUBLIC, Prose Poems and Poetics from California (anthology): Los Angeles
Best New Poets 2008 (anthology): It's Snowing in Santiago de Chuco
Buffalo Carp: 40
California Quarterly: This is the Last Day of Most of Your Life
Cold Mountain Review: 1947
The Decadent Review: Hunting
Faultline: Uncle Patrick
Freefall: Sleep Where You Happen to Lie
Hiram Poetry Review: 1968
The Hollins Critic: Lament of Finoozeh Dumas
Homage to Vallejo (anthology): Photograph Found Between the Pages of *Los Heraldos Negros*
The Main Street Rag: Loitering in Lima
Off the Coast: Juarez, Mexico
Pearl: What Your Dad's Underpants Have to Do With Space Travel
The Pinch: Les Bêtes Feroces
Poetry International: You are Walking in Circles in the Desert
The Prairie Journal: The Silence of the Trees
Red Wheelbarrow: Corporate Casualties
Taj Mahal Review: Wally Pugmire
The Tulane Review: Meditation On Baked Goods
The William and Mary Review: A Parade in Galway
The Zodiac Review: A Well Preserved Man

Thanks to Tonia Cheong for her continued love, support, and understanding, and for her edits.

CONTENTS

Lament of Finoozeh Dumas

It struck—like fission at the core—that he was an ordinary man with
no historic mission, no destiny to fulfill, not even a moment when
the masses would say

yes, for that instant, we saw the pinnacle of Man in all his idiopathic
brilliance

and the stars were confetti and the nation changed.
Possible, indeed. An ordinary man with extraordinary sympathy for
himself.

You are Walking in Circles in the Desert

What a shame, you said, holding a match to the bed,
which burned like a woman in heat,
these possessions betray me, I hate them.

Your home was in ruins—burned, smashed up.

The sofa will not stay true, nor will fifty pistols
or a shoe…

You'd quit your job, closed accounts, divorced M.

You walked in circles in the desert
because the straight way had proved untrue.

Alonso, I tried to disagree
but lost my hat in the wind.

We can no longer cleave to the sheets in despair.

The world suffers intolerable hunger.
The world which fed us for years.

They see your shadow on the crestline.

I'm coming to the Valley of the Kings,
with wine to tenderize, and twenty nine prayers.

Pain

came to the room, hollowed out like a razor shell. Small, with big
hands, a bum hip. Stood in the doorway, elbow on the frame,
fiddling with a hinge. Smelled like spoiled plums. Went by
Traspaso. Could have been from Brooklyn. "Are you a ghost?"

I got no friends and reams of enemies.
Doctors, for one, in their ice-cream suits,

but I been here from the jump, before medicine.
People hate me worse than death itself.

Why? they keep asking.
Why anything? I exist, it's a fact.

Nobody tries to snuff out funhouses, right?
They throw poisons at me—salts, pills, drinks.

The healers are the worst.
Buggin' killers if you ask me.

Nobody done me in yet, but think they sing
my praises in church? No, they call me vile crap,

or it's "From Depths of Woe I Cry to Thee"
and don't get me started on the blues.

Not once has nobody asked how I'm feeling.
Well, I'm hurtin' some but I'll survive.

Here and There

Here is a house
pets
work
bills
tomorrow &

                                        there
                                        what's there
                                        you ask

that which

                                        is not

here but

                                        here

my
like leaping
over

                    meadows
                    solar winds
                    rings of
                    fire &
                    ice

can one
go

                                        back

& forth

who's
to say
the weight
does not
give way
I've been

    here not

                    here
                    &
                    again

    here

OK praise
civic lawns
good credit
the commissioner of baseball
but once
you're

        here

here
is kind
of a drag
&

                    here
                    is of
                    significance.

Stinkthing

Into the water, down to the feathery loam
of lake whatever.

3:14 a.m. Education, experience: irrelevant.
Dimensions, temperature, wildlife… blah blah, better
to make contact, like a child, a leaf.

Let the game ignoramus pioneer.

The stinging divide—very very deep,
cold as soda,
the fish with knives in her mouth dreams freaky dreams.

What else? Like diving to the bottom of time.

Back on land, a sodden stinkthing moving
through the suburbs, I seem to haunt the fenced-in dogs.

Bleeding Witches

If sleep is a kind of dying and waking a rebirth,
what do you call midnight-to-dawn
and those who wander in it?
The Hour of the Ticks and Flares,
The Rise of the Bleeding Witches,
The Wrath of the Butcherbirds?
Uncle Jimmy used to say, *Monkey see, monkey don't,*
which is not wise but has its perks,
weaving through the mausoleums of the city,
all the corpses,
all the promise.

Dr. Lindquist

It's five hundred years from now. Changes in communication,
commerce.
The tattoo? As obsolete as Washington's wig.
Hip hop? Zzzzz. Neil deGrass Tyson's a crackpot.

Students find history a bore but adore a profane scholar
with a spotted scalp who lectures, for kicks,
on public bathrooms of the 21st century.

"Note the tissue, perforated in sensible sections, the automated,
weight-sensitive, hands-off flushers. The sensory faucets, a flood-
proof sprig for the palm, no more! Air dryers so they wouldn't go
mad with the towels."

Laughter, texting. It's good to be the furthest point
on the evolutionary line.
Who's more out of style than the dead?

"Smartphones, AI, drones, they're only part of the story.
"The johns round out The Age of Technology.
"These people couldn't be trusted to shit properly."

What Your Dad's Underpants Have to Do With Space Travel

Been thinking of the astronaut who drifted away
in his capsule, still drifting in the huge space out there,
part of a loop. Ninety four years old,
gone bony, brain splat on the steel hatch,
mouth in a slush, thighs running around the cabin.
Written off by the Russian government in 1960.
Nobody wants to think of him this way. It's better
not to think of some things, like your dad's underpants.
Where is the good in my dad's underpants? you ask,
and what's it got to do with astronauts?
Which reminds me: He must have been wearing underwear.
It's not all about radar, physics, launch angles.
Nobody wants to admit that sad diaper was loosed
on the universe, but it was, an artifact
of the human race, and they'll draw conclusions, you know.

A Chunk of Cereal Pops Into the Eye of Godse Gopal

A bride
says *I do*
I can't
cries a priest
in Sicily
who dies
of scleroderma

Three warehouse workers
gather
in a pub
in Kilarney
one tells jokes
one digs in
his ear
one goes
to the
pisser
six times

A closet prophet
ignoring the *taptap*
of his wife
considers time

A Moscow scholar opts for cryogenics
"to be thawed out when people are kinder"

George Bush is planning
to shadow-box
on Saturday
Joan Baez
secretly

misses
Vietnam
Mike Tyson's
been reading
The Captain's Verses

Mrs. Pryor's
Pekinese
sneezes
thirteen times
Mr. Pryor
has a
bad case
of the jim jams
"In the next life
I would like
to be a pea" he says

A mockingbird
spends the summer
scaring
sparrows
then arrives
for eight seconds
of love
or rape
it's hard
to tell
which

"So much for rubber"
Dave tells the Wichita moon
"Dave's lost his mind"
Dave's boss tells a friend
at the coffee pot

"He's moving to
the Sierras with $1,600
and a tent"

At the bottom
of the Black Sea
a sea-sponge
overeats
overhead
two boaters
argue
the merits
of Kawakami's
Breasts and Eggs

A chunk
of cereal
pops
into
the eye
of Godse Gopal
across the street
it rains
on all four feet
of Lowell Gomes
while he
washes
his Tesla

A peepul tree
in Nepal
falls
killing one dreamy boy

Saddam Hussein's jailer

swears he was
tender
with his bluebells

On a starlit esplanade
in Evans Indiana
four souls
gather in a breadfruit tree
As of Tuesday
Pham Lee Linda and Jorge
can be described
as indescribable
and you

Rootless

What if a tree gets severed from its roots,
splits at the crotch into legs and
ganglia grows: fruits, flowers, leaves,
which could be called mouth-like, sex-like, nerve-like?
And branching from the spine, the thicket,
as complex as Ang Lee's brain,
perceives the world and being in it?
What if the tree walks around the city
that way, brilliant but rootless,
and the night is immense?

Letter From a Dead Man Who Was Uncommonly Quiet

Flies, I waved them off
but they boomeranged back.
They loved me;
I loathed them.

Birds swooned in the sky
like fathers
of the flies.

The people wished to fly too.
They hovered,
pecked, stung.

At night, when I sought solitude,
the phone rang,
a skunk peered in,

car alarms, crickets,
hinges, winds,
all the pretty screaming.

Stranger, friend,

my life was not mine
and everyone knew it
but me.

Loitering in Lima

What's with the Borselino,
the alligator shoes? Who wears a silk-
blend suit in 95-degree heat?
Loitering in Lima on a bench
between two putrescent corpses.
Maybe he's next and knows it
here in *centro,* a long way from L.A.,
in the fractured shadows of cathedrals.
Look how tender he is with *Trilce's* spine.
You decide: Is this a suicide or *revolucion?*

1947

After taking the Northern Pacific, you uncleft from commerce and
walked beneath the arc lamps with a book of Mai-Yao Chen's
poems in your pocket. You figured your generation, coming off the
big war, would change the way the world worked. The war, as they
say, was an organized bore, and we hadn't yet learned of the
Milgram experiment. Two saw-whet owls in the laurel tree mirrored
the big-eyed dreams of ordinary men, and from a distance, the faint
smells of camphor and gentian. Gone were the sedgy ponds of the
south, the constraints of pubescence. It was time to buy a house and
put a television in, fill bookcases. You walked the streets that night
and your heart was a cocky toad. When you passed a window, you
looked at your reflection and saw a young man with the future
opening like a maw. That was before more wars, a divorce, layoffs,
night sweats, before the cold scalp and reed-thin thighs, before you
had to hire a kid to mow your lawn. You were masterless then. My,
how you were masterless.

Ways to Pass the Night

I.
Call ex-girlfriends, ex-boyfriends, confess to all your lies.
Tell them love was never fully there
but never went away.

II.
Immured in the closet,
read Act III of Antigone.

III.
Drink eggnog; leave a little on your lip, talk
to possums about the limits of language,
the chief cause of astonishment.

IV.
Bake two torts and a lime pie
for the beetles on the hill.

V.
Make a pyre of your best shoes;
the higher the fire, the greater the relief.
Sprint across the embers in your last pair.

Falling
And when the earth shall claim your limbs,
then shall you truly dance—Kahlil Gibran

You want to fall from city hall, all the jaundice, lord, they're dying
in those suits, dying without permits. Soto, McOsker, Heather Hutt.
No amount of propaganda, no code or law, can stop it. They'll be
recalled for unfilled potholes and the spread of the weed. You want
to fall from Bunker Hill because it's trying to be perfect. It won't
stand, it can't. The bank tower, the music hall, the glass and steel
and brick… you want to fall from Union Station, fall off the wheels
of speed, curve into the countryside. You want to fall from
Hollywood, Skid Row, Central Market, the heavy, the light, the
infirm, the infants, the working girls. You want to lie down in a 10th
Street park, freefalling upside-down within, unweaving from the
skin.

The Silence of the Trees

I tried to fall from the mind,
which banked to Tangier, to Galilee, to Hook Road,

and now I've flown the bed and flits about the breeze
on Coyote Hill.

It's 2:20 a.m.,
twilight in Taipei.

The silence of the trees—a lair for the lun-
                                                atic fringe:

the owl who thinks he's Bly, the addled wren,
the red-eyed, paranoid, root-hugging nymphs.

The cicada shed her see-through shell
and quit the life of flying.

Down That Way

Melatonin, Tylenol PM, and Ambien
were no match for the mind and fifty minutes of skull chatter—
why the judenfrei, the Mao famine, King Ashoka—

was enough so I rose
from the low bed, took to the alleys of Shandong,
came upon a shed and

gathered there, miles from the dynasts in Beijing,
corn farmers, cabbies, and leathermen
bet their earnings on a cricket-singing contest,

coaxing the creatures with wisps of boiled hay.
I threw in fifteen yuan on a sonorous blotch
who, Mr. Liu told me, was trained to fight for money

in the Tang tradition but only sang.
"The fighting is down that way or… do you like singing better?"
And I, an American at war overseas and at home—

in the city, the stomach—smiled and said,
"Yeah, yeah, tonight I do."

Photograph Found Between the Pages of *Los Heraldos Negros*

This man, I want to call him Cesar, but can't say, down in Lima
with a flute and skinned chicken on his back. 1930s?
I can't say, except he wears a suit, it could be wool,
with buttons on the cuffs, a kerchief in the pocket,
he's too young for the cane, which he leans on,
so serious, circling himself like an ailing fish.

The townsfolk are poor; they kill
because they prize their sisters.
The back-turned roads are slick with mud.
That summer, a bird sleeps through a revolution,
a girl in a stitched dress struts for olives,
and nine children starve like dogs.

Cesar, tell us about *Nativa,* your mother, the fires rolling
in the windows on Hotel Street, the song whistling
from your flute,
in the 1930s, in a suit.
Tell us of your sorrows, tell us of the rain.

Boxes

Keep away all boxes. The cedar trunk with its tree smell. The
ringholder bedded in velvet. Pink buildings with deco art and
hanging plants. Tuck-tops, boxboards, gables, clamshells. One day
they will box my mother in a wound in the ground, grass trimmed to
frame her body, as if the whole were contained.

Wally Pugmire

Propped against a wall, headphones on, cap tipped over his eyes,
lunch at his side, thoughts of wharves, bulkheads, and the state of
the maritime industry as it relates to the Port of Rotterdam rests
Wally Pugmire who never needed much.

He dreams of military juntas, pranks, space travel. The wind undoes
his newspaper, sending it cartwheeling across the docks. He was
reading about the Kuiper Belt, and the gridded pictographs of Latin
American artists.

This plays out to Drake. There's a rhythm to the business of moving
goods. The geometry of Rotterdam is an industrial wonder. A clean
green apple is a neat trick of evolution and a salami sandwich a
testament to man.

He sleeps because he stays up late mixing paints and watching
Sumo on You Tube. If some long lost friend or second cousin asks
say there against the wall rests Wally Pugmire who never needed
much.

This Kind of Thing Should Take Place in Catalonia, or
Alexandria, or at the Wailing Wall

You're an American with a tinge of guilt in the pancreas
and a sense, between the third and fourth ribs, that somewhere
a ceremony's going on.

Just last week, a Dallas CEO rammed a knife in his groin.
A Camden man drove for days with his mortal infant.

It could happen anywhere, anytime. Austin, Chicago, a feed lot in
Des Moines.
All we need is a charismatic and a crowd.

For now, we'll call it The Public Cleansing of Tear Ducts or
The Salving of Blisters, Thrashes and Cancers.

As usual, the cock and the ox are imperiled. Clouds amass like
brigades. What was of much importance once is of no importance
now.

No Other Way

The old problem: You're not prepared to die, you can't sleep,
you're anchored here.
Walking helps. You seem to be of some importance outdoors.
A village of leaves riots; you're roundly condemned by the birds.
Ponzi schemes in back rooms. Exotic, symbolic shadows.
These are the nights you think of the sorrowful Jesus.
At Gethsemane. he fell on his face. *Let this cup pass* from me.
No, no, no other way. You must be sacrificed.
Forget pride. Weep.
Forget long life. Learn to be kind.

Sleep Where You Happen to Lie

Maybe if you run and keep running, past the county line. That's it,
run to exhaustion,
fall in a heap,
sleep where you happen to lie.

If you're stabbed in the spleen and robbed of your wallet, so be it,
more time to rest,
you bested the bank, left the boss in a bind.
Run until your lungs explode. Up ahead—a mulch bed, a tree of
birds.

The masses fan out, encircle. A leopard in Kenya cries because
she's missing out,
a legless man in Leeds dreams of marathons.
Where you land intrigues a million insects.
You couldn't care less what time it is, the time is always now.

Run until the mind lags and the eyes split open like grapes.
Sleep where you happen to lie.

Uncle Patrick

After the wake for his wife, we've come to the end of the jetty to
summon the Furies. A fisherman gathers line lengths from his reel
and a gorged cormorant sleeps in a scoop of granite.

I'm thirteen; flags of tissue flap from the nicks in my neck and he
tells a story: Cronus taking a blade to Uranus, a rusty shower falling,
quenching some eternal thirst in the sea, and then Tisiphene,
Allecto, Maguera and all their sisters since, including Jan, who, he
says, was forgiving, a kind of divine redemption.

As I finger my cuts and, below, the detritus of county folk—
bottles, bags, a hankie—rocks to the rhythm of the tides, he slides a
nipper from his vest and grins the grin of timely ideas: *I'm going to
have a drink. You just stand there and bleed awhile.*

AA Whale Watching Trip

A skein of snow
falls from Mt. Antonio,

rain falls,
streams and rivers fall,

seeds fall from phoebes,
to bracken and broom,

lovers to the waist
of desire,

seabirds and senior citizens
from struggle,

politicians from drowsy integrity,
into monied sleep.

In the capital, freedom falls
into fascism's arms,

present falls to past
and leaves

something new
to live up to

for the wrecked and ragged
on a cold boat

in a Baja lagoon,
and calves fall

from their mamas
and forge north.

Wonderful

"Float above the facts"—Emerson

You return to the word *comfort.*
The vicars of Christ
convene
down the street

Hawking's
tired tomes
tilt
on shelves

you prayed
you read
you thought
you shat

it's 10:16 p.m.
how old are you
now
papa's gone

you're uncomfortable
terminally
eternally
grateful for

Borges and
and your blue room
that's OK
you're a cliché

but you can
get flotational

can't you
on Sangiovese

talk out loud
to outliers
Moliere
Voltaire

laugh at the loon
crying poor
in the leaves
look

Venus moves
past the moon
peach on blue and
and you can wonder
after all.

Les Betes Feroces

In the crawling light of dawn, dogs bark
and down below, terror. You know madness

crashing through teeth. The mind says *just dogs*
yet all your nerves are Krakow Jews.

In a past life you tromped across a blood-brown tundra
or fell in the fold-up way of the caribou.

Memory's a silly thing in the new life, isn't it?
But a fact more absolute than God.

A man is allowed to shiver in bed,
reach for eyewear,

muse on the gingko tree
or the souls of corpses

convening say, in Fresno,
beneath a parking lot.

Until that day, you say, we are all
les betes feroces or caribou

so you stuff your pockets with biscuits
and go where the grapes grow

and migrant women bend at the waist.

How to Pay Tribute to the Self

A yaktail for a beard and a skull bowl stinking of beans.
That's what it takes. And sliders, serape, a mandolin,
a pitchy *happy deathday* to your grandpa.

Then they'll perk up when you ask: "Who feels my pain but me?"
Your koan in response to Hume, your paean to self.

It helps to be asexual. Things to drop in: Monism, Goethe's botany,
an old family recipe for chicken stew.

Always look for bargains, always return
to that infected root

with a wink and spin, and when you sing out,
never, under any circumstances, expect a response.

This is the Last Day of Most of Your Life

There comes a time when the future you looked to with thoughts of
lord-knows-what
becomes an artifact of the mind.

You're standing there, the shadow long;
now the light's on a boy whose pants don't fit.

No doubt about it, it's getting cold. You shuck to
where the light was but off to Falls Canyon or Tokyo it goes

and there you are with your feet, knees, thumbs, lips,
with your odd head, and what now?

The Wait

Coyote Hill, the high point of the city. If God comes to Fullerton, he
comes here.
A good place to start a flood. The coyotes, thin and gray,
feeding on the ribs of a kill, look up like criminals.
"I am not the chief of police," I tell them.
I'm waiting, like the weeping tree, the screech owl.
All of life is a wait pretending to be this or that.
We should not feel badly for the cat lying there sacrificed.

1973

A cul-de-sac in the oven-hot Pomona Valley. Flat roofs, white-rock
gardens, station wagons. Saturday morning, the sounds of Soul
Train, the silhouette of
Lynn Dixie dancing in a window.

I moved like a beached sea crab. Cesar said on the day he was born
God was sick, and God,
who spent the Vietnam and Nixon years at *Carnival,* was sick again;
his offspring breathed
the sickness in.

The street was ringed with fiddling, pre-cancerous fathers and their
kids.
Ron Jansen, high on weed, sicced his trained crow on the necks
of his brothers, and the crow spasmed and cackled.

I was mostly slow, I came to see, slower than Wallace, who tromped
on Miss Dixie's dichondria, slower than a bush plane, wheels,
water, light, slower than some unseen thing dogging me all spring
and into adolescence.

40

Jogging in the hills of La Habra. On one side,
PE students on a field of grass; they look like spastic jelly beans.

On the other, an old man sweeping a sidewalk.
Monday morning, damp, the sound of breath, a breath that is not mine,

coming in, going out. Red leaves, yellow leaves, parrots in the yew tree.
Fourteen things to do today, large and small.

The children see me pass, too far to taunt.
The man looks up from his aura of dust and nods.

Misdemeanors

In my pockets a poppy, a walnut, a blue stone,
gathered on the road to nowhere, I don't know why,
and can't decide what they mean, if anything.
Unpaid bills and breakups
like hawks circle back and hover.
I no longer shoo the birds.
My silence, a shadow, is a hiding place for others.
It's 3 a.m. on Pico Road; I'm creeping out the rats.
Someone should call the cops, shine a light in my eye.
I'm dying to empty these pockets of clues.

Corporate Casualties

drinking at a bar in Long Beach
6 weeks after
the company
laid off
35
there's 1
hey
hey
I buy him a rum & coke
any prospects?
looks
calls
makes his pitch
52
2 decades on the job
200 sick days
unused
heard anything? could you put a word in?
no & yes
1 drink only
& he'd like to get the tip please
more perplexed than pissed off
20 more days & he loses the house

Gasoline and Daffodils

You're filling up in West Covina, or Boise, or Baltimore,
wherever you happen to be.
$4.56 a gallon, something like that.

A day like any day: warm, clear, tanned hills,
two clouds—one a scruff,
the other slick as a blimp's back.

The smell of fuel. You think of fire, Iraq, ancient lakes.
Three feet away, a wood box of flowers; you bury
your nose in the bouquet.

A horn blows or a phone rings or the nozzle clicks
so you head to work or the market or lunch
and that's how it goes,

gasoline and daffodils,
something to keep you going,
something to make you stop.

Son, Brother, Lover, Fool

That night, reflecting on the day—
coffee and funnies, two insults,
decisions, loose ends,
the rapiers, the ensouled,
my performance—

I went to the pond and the pond-weeds,
dodged a squalid man,
plucked a mudleaf,
pondered its *foliage architecture*
and my own mitochondria.

I was Homosapien, privileged in the outer purlieus of London;
son, brother, lover, fool, a freakish shape within a bigger freakish
shape;
feaster feasting on avocados, ginseng, Lorca; star-stuff and star-
struck;
lost, conflicted, a love/hate relationship with the brain: all day
I cheered its creative ways then… fury on a pillow.

It dawned that it tried
to con me
that it was me
but it wasn't, nor the big dog of reality.
It was locomotive; it steered or got steered.

What, then, was I?
Light broke through the trees
and scattered and ran
like bits of gold, rivulets of piss.
The fractured couldn't be tallied.

It's Snowing in Santiago de Chuco

and no one can believe it,
not the lonesome, backroad dogs or the insane.
The stars blew up, says a man stand-
ing at the window in his socks. The world is changing;
those twins, hope and dread, snip each others' wounds
and show them off in vases. The vases are clay
and the earth is breaking off in pieces.
Cesar Vallejo is dead, technically,
non-ambulatory, not there in a winged-back chair
in a book-filled room, but it's snowing
in Santiago de Chuco, and no one can believe it.

One Hundred Million Years

A bench beneath a pine tree in Puerto Real. A clock showed noon—
time to break for the labors of mankind,
for the bronze era, farms, quarries, shipyards,
Baltimore, Long Beach, Texas City.

The Man with a Hoe was singing. Anvils, hooks, and hard drives
burned in a goo.
A fruit picker asked his sister for a Band-Aid. An engineer removed
her glasses.
Cesar Chavez and Bernie Sanders were taking selfies.

The human queue stretched to the sun.
A dead ringer for Salvadore Novo stood on the steps of the old
church
and said, "That's it. There's nothing left to do."

Tabasco Estada

The cow—overeater, sad-sack napper—moped along.
Flies realized her pacifism.

All she wanted was tree-shade,
a patch of green, a patch of peace across the road.

Made eye contact with no one
(straight-ahead gaze, no trouble thank you).

A speeding jeep to the ribs
excited the birds, the leaves.

The driver, a neat, forward man, caressed the hood
and cursed her shattered there in the sun.

Juarez, Mexico

The wettest winter in years. Shallow graves slip-slide downslope,
into the muddy ravine, and the vendors are ragged as goats.

This is the year of the Big Dodge, the High Collar, the Cursed Boot,
the year the butcher mauls his cat to pay the rent.

Cecilio: "Where did all the goddamn flour go?"
Margarita: "Perhaps we are being tested."

The bouganvillea bloom sooner than expected, a fruit picker leaves
his wife,
teenage boys flee to Yuma, Arizona and

a nameless Edith Piaf
belts out *songs of the revolution.*

That was years ago. Only those who are made of wood,
like desert trees, remember.

"Maria, maybe?" says a man splayed on the steps of his porch.
"They smashed her violin."

"It was a handmade flute," says his brother.
They agree on this: two boys used a coffin for a sled and were
lashed with a rope,

and crowds amassed beneath the terrace on Friday nights to forget,
for an hour or two, about weather and food.

Round the World

When it's 3:12 a.m. and you can't sleep
you go to the store for bread and juice
because you're alive
and have to eat

and sometimes

you swipe a yo-yo
to pass the hours
before daybreak.

Meditation On Baked Goods

The hottest March 10 in Los Feliz history and you're focused on a
baker's apron.
It's cool in here, the coins in your pocket are cooling, biscuits sound
good to go
with your iced tea.

You don't shy from the scut and scat of shoes or a gum-chomping
branch manager
who, on another day, might make you burn around the ears.
No, you feel too cool, too good. Moments ago you were

blinded by the sidewalk, irked each time you passed a news rack,
caught the news
and, somehow, applied it to your life. But now, eyeing the patch of
sleet falling
from the baker's knees, you're thinking of biscuits.

The Milkweed Man

At 35, he made 50K a year,
at 40, more, at 44, a little more—
he was always 10K away,
a pivot point from his
stocks zooming up.

2:18 a.m. There are skeins
of wooly pod milkweed
in the meadow—
who could resist?
It healed the Ohlones, the Choctaws.

Ratepayers,
don't get The Milkweed Man wrong.
Nobody questions
your lack of wooly pod
and we know dough leavens or flattens.

In five hours, he's off
to work a union job,
pay off his truck—a yeoman
with a back ache
(that's what it takes).

Earning and yearning
are cousins with secrets
though too much
and you're walking
the blistered streets,

dogs hoarse from moaning.
They sound like you feel
but a little less free.

You decide the price,
put what you must do here ________________.

A Well Preserved Man

In the bogs of County Sligo, worms curl around corpses like pasta.
Around the corner, in a gray house with a red door, a family mourns
a missing man. Who knows how they'll feel from one minute to the
next. The man's wife, Sara, says he's in a better place, as if saying it
makes it true, but why question the faith that gets her up at dawn?
She served breakfast today as Uncle Ted quoted Tagore to two kids
eating black pudding and potato farls. Theirs is a childhood without
dad, the hunter who kept a taut bow and talked of retiring to
Garristown. He's been gone two years. Sundays are for stories and
prayers. If we could only tell them that there in the peat lies a well
preserved man who laughed at his mishap, that he was true to his
vows. If worms had ears we'd urge them to go easy, stay out of the
eye sockets. Thomas is meat beneath the rain-damp grass. Sara
plays a game of tug-of-war, her mood ribboned on a rope, but one-
in-a-million are good enough odds to tighten the hold.

1968
with thanks to Buddy Wakefield...

The folks return from drinking Blinkers and Red Hooks at Gold
Dust Lounge in Union Square. Mother wears a nipped-waist skirt
and cat's-eye glasses, dad's in a skinny tie and loafers. Their
colleagues, cursing Nixon, pour from decanturs and at five I get
the urge for change but forty four years later they know better, I
know better, we don't talk politics and war, it's about oxygen
tanks and low-sodium diets because the revolutionaries and their
son, who's just trying to get by, sense, after decades of unrest,
election let-downs, and personal loss we're coping with what
Teddy Roosevelt saw in his day: "There are certain hideous sights
which once seen can never be erased from the mental retina," and I
wish a Steinem-esque woman or one of those men who could win
a war and also fix the Ford would walk in but instead I declare,
"Forgiveness is the release of all hope for a better past,"
"Onward," mother says, father nods, we all half-believe and it's
just enough.

Faculty Party, Saranac Lake

Look at the dog, digging, digging,
failing to break ground. His name
is Freckles, we're told, a little longhair
longing for the other side of the door.
Too short and no opposable thumb
so he plays to his strengths and wrecks
the floor. Because you can open
the door, you're God. Because he's here,
heaven is out there. A snack can't sate him,
nor a slow cat, though it would help for
a spell. It comes down to that door,
and all the humans are howling.

Devoured in La Paz

I.
The froth of the bay comes
laving over the city.
Trash and mud. Sea scum.
A smirking scat ray
kicked around the streets.

II.
What is it you say,
seven echoes from your birth?
You want a Japanese lover,
a parrot confidante?

III.
America's doing standup,
Europe's in the sauce,
Baja's
the gimpy leg
of a dog named Kona.

IV.
Midnight,
relentless rain,
not a doctor in sight.
You are not the master
of your own shoes even.

V.
Devoured in La Paz
in the season of the whales,
pity the skin/grist/teeth,
praise what remains.

Hunting

The fact is I think I am a verb instead of a personal pronoun. A verb is anything that signifies to be; to do; or to suffer. I signify all three—Ulysses S. Grant

Bushkill, Pennsylvania. The doe and her fawn
from the shagbark
emerge

forty yards
from Ed,
who lifts his flintlock,

fires into mama's flank.
We converge on her clawing the muck,
eyeing the run-offs, suckling air.

The scholar with his peccadilloes
pulls out a flask of tea,
takes a hit, hands it to me.

It feels like eons
since Troy, Antietam, Vietnam '66.
"You botched the kill," he tells Ed,

wipes the tea from his chin,
freshens the powder
in the frizzen,

retracts the lever and—
non ignara mali, miseris succurrere disco—
lets her have it: a minie ball in the heart.

Sweet Success

All the others were only displeased
with trivial segments, carped non-
sensically about nonsense—Natasha

You should be here, Nat,
in the heart
of the San Gabriel Valley
at a forty thousand-circ paper
in the milieu
of the 21st century
they bitch about
rain
traffic
and you should
see the celebrations
desserts
some sort of raffle
Sweet Success
a banner reads
no workplace accidents
in July
which saved the boss
who laid off
fifteen
in June
tens of thousands of dollars
in workers comp
that's the hell
of it
the workers party
as the rich get richer
and they do it

with cups
of butternut ice cream

Father, 1975

He's in the garage reviving a pea-green, 1966 Mustang
with 200,000 miles on her. Someone drove her cross-country five
times.
The sod of Middle America clings like fungus to the wheel-wells,
the engine chokes with emphysema.

He's a mechanic's son from South Bend, Indiana,
whose politics can be summed up as pro little guy.
He likes the garage, where he can right wrongs,
take a no-hope Ford and make her run again.

He's been sweating and cursing for weeks;
on this Sunday morning we emerge—
she's humming, man—and cut off
a Mercedes-Benz SEL 6.9

and the driver, wearing a USC cap, flips us the bird
and my father smiles and tells me, "Always pull
in front of the high-priced ones,
they have more to lose than we do."

Los Angeles

Down where the sludge pools between mudstone rocks and cats
prowl beneath the river bridge, I think of buried churches, Juanenos,
meat feasts. The flotsam of the city floats by—a milk carton sucked
dry, a Halloween mask. The trees on San Pedro, condemned against
the walls of the Toy District, might be blindfolded, given cigarettes.
The rain tree with its lean body and beaming corsage is a girl stood
up on prom night. Skid row smells like downtown's crotch. "The
president's an asshole," says a voice in a cardboard box. The souls
of Angelenos, the rumor goes, get sold at Central Market, and look
at this—a Walgreens across the street from a CVS. Sorties the size
of tic-tacs get dropped on the Capitol Self. Rail story on page 1 of
the *L.A. Times:* An oil plant lights up the Eboch delta, sickening
crops. Two blocks away, flies feast on the moist parts of children.
We in Los Feliz, Boyle Heights, Bel-Air, and Watts could commit
to putting out the fire. The movement would be called Enough or
Because or Why Not. Thumbing through Huxley, Fante, Wanda
Coleman, but not Sartre, Shakespeare, or James, what do they know
of the mood of Fifth Avenue? Evening on Bunker Hill. Who but the
loon calls it a night? A woman in Pradas bumps her way through.
Who named the stars? Some see a badge up there, an earring, a
torch, a buckle, a geyser, a blemish, lost teeth, seashells. Enough in-
between episodes of mankind, dramatized on TV. Bird anthems and
lettuce in the compost concern us now. On to the pueblo to buy a
stone bowl to eat from, to give *Mision Capilla del Santisimo* a try,
to heed the madres who teach us how to care and don't get elected.
In the end, stricken with dead legs and cotton-mouth, in a crossway
of jabber-gesticulation, wouldn't we meld in their arms forever?
Escort them from their pueblos, bungalows, tents and wicky huts,
their pied-a-terres, to Plaza de Los Angeles. Usher the shy one in the
lamplight, grooming her zarape. Bring them en masse to this city of
commerce.

Doing Time

No conflicts, no pressing matters, drowsy and you still can't sleep.
Past problems persist, you guess, a karmic cause for this effect. You
were a mutt who fell asleep on watch, let's say,
robbers stepped over your heaving chest, slit the necks of ten men.
You woke to a stir in camp, pawed your snotty eyes. The captain
wacked your rump; this didn't signal breakfast.
Tears, disbelief. You looked up with a rumpled ear, wondered what
the fuss was.

A Parade in Galway

Hungover from those oil-dark pints of Guinness, I drove from Cork
to a parade in Galway but did not ask why they cheered in the
streets, imagining, instead, that that day, miles from the buried
cannons in the cliffs of Kerry and a half-day removed from what I
witnessed at that pub—the pallor of a horseman's face and in the
barmaid's shoes a certain discontent—we'd see the Second Coming.
That would explain the beggar quoting Ovid, the kettledrums, and
one naked man, balls bobbing like peaches on a vine, diving into the
JFK fountain. That, not some rugby scrum, would explain away my
headache, my heartache, and make a buoy of my soul, so I thought
that way until I rose the next morning, made my way through the
fog and salted myself, like a limbed egg, like food for a higher kind,
in the sea.

A Day In the Life of Nicky Chi

Morning
He wakes ill, unsure he can do it.
The day, that is.
Dawn, like flashlights, creeps through slats,
he's bumping about, no time to sort out
what just happened, or didn't.
It's off to work

in a spread collar and eyeglasses,
with jokes for coworkers
and donuts for Lori in HR.
Movement earns him mercy
for an hour.
Mr. Chi is a medical coder.

Afternoon
His heart is a tom drum
as he trick-or-treats for Dr. Vaughn.
"Some good days, some rough, the Klonopin evens things out,
but without sleep…" And *yesss,* here come the scripts.
Klonopin gets him through a.m., wine to 10,
Ambien through closing time.

Night
He endured the landlord; it's on
to soup, his horn,
a newspaper story on the Platte County Steam Engine Show.
All day, he felt like a tag-sale trinket,
to be valued
in, say, 2088.

Time for an Irish exit to the barn.
"I write from a hole in the haymow I dug."

His memoir is too long and not very good.
He sleeps with a note in his ear.
It reads, "The performance is over."

www.ingramcontent.com/pod-product-compliance
Lightning Source LLC
LaVergne TN
LVHW090220180726
843492LV00012B/2604

9 788196 202613